Fore

I lie on my back on top of th
served as my bed. I remember my c
except for the small light from the k
shadows from whatever motion was outside. I had just added
minutes to my prepaid Tracphone and I listened intently as my new
friend vividly told me the story of her son's death. I addressed it as
death but from the very start of our time together she never called it
"death" or said "my son died"; No, "my son was murdered" she said
with such strength and conviction that to be totally honest my very
initial thought was that she was lying. "Who can lose a child and in
such a way, and tell that story with absolutely no emotion?" What I
then thought was void of emotion was actually strength, and as our
time together increased that is one of the main factors that captivated
me about Rhonda Lynette Russell who is now Rhonda Lynette
Broux, my wife. We have grown to share a life together and she is
undoubtedly my best friend, but as close as we are, the one thing that
we don't share is the feeling and knowing of the deep pain of losing
a child; and the God's honest truth is I wouldn't want to become
familiar with such pain, because I doubt I would have the courage or
tenacity that my wife has.

Brandon Chatman is a person I never met. I am sure that in
this small city of Baton Rouge we probably crossed paths and maybe
talked to each other briefly, but I never knew the young man in life.
However, at the risk of seeming dramatic, I have encountered his
spirit on more than one occasion. He has let me know that his energy
still exists, not in a theatrical ghost story sort of way, but through
little noises, shadows, and other friendly awarenesses that have let
me become familiar with him and thankfully the fact that he
approves of me in his mom's life. As for Rhonda, I know she has a
gift, and that God has ordained her to use her gift to help others.

Unfortunately the trauma of losing our kids to homicide seemingly has become a tragic part of our cultural fabric. Rhonda's story of loss and the finding of peace is an example that proves God's love and power is tangible and real, and not just some abstract notion. Peace is possible and the book you hold is my wife's personal account of the process. We hope and pray that others who have suffered a great loss as such will find comfort in the fact that there is someone who has experienced that ultimate loss, and while my wife isn't claiming expertise, she is merely saying "hey, I feel your pain. I understand. Let me tell you what helped me". I hope the sincerity of her spirit to help resonates from these pages and into your hearts.

J. Broux, Author
"A Hazy Shade of Faith"

Dedication

First, this book is dedicated to the memory of my wonderful, loving son, Brandon Dwayne Chatman, who lost his life at the age of 19 to a senseless murder. My undying, immeasurable love for you gave me initial inspiration to write this book, so that even in death you will continue to touch many lives across the world, bringing good to the hearts of others as you loved to do. Like your gentle, sweet spirit, your beautiful memory will live on for forever.

Brandon Dwayne Chatman

January 2, 1986 – July 6, 2005

To my wonderful sons Damon Christopher Chatman, and Justin Latrell Russell, who've been right with me, helping me to keep it together while also persevering, though enduring their own pain of the loss of their big brother, whom they too loved dearly: It was because of you two that I even had the desire to live through this, and it's because of your selflessness and support that I am able to tell this story. I am so proud of and thankful for both of you, and I love you madly.

To my mother(Linda Tolbert-Mosley), my grandmother(Lena Tolbert), my aunt/Brandon's godmother(Cynthia Bienemy) and my aunt(Shelia (Shenia) Noah): I dedicate this book to you because you stuck by me, prayed for me, and cushioned and insulated me, shielding me through this though your own hearts were torn apart as well. I couldn't have made it without you. I love and treasure you all.

To Brandon's father, Alphonse Dwayne Chatman, his grandmother, Mrs. Norma Reed, his sisters Keia and Ciera Chatman, his brother Terrell Chatman, and all the **many** other family members and friends who loved him, and whose hearts were broken due to his death. May you find joy in knowing that through this book, the memories of his life and death will go on to bless the hearts of countless others, just as he did.

To my indescribable best friend, confidante, supporter and soul mate; my loving husband, Jason Lamar Broux, Sr. As I pondered over how I can help others in my position, you said "get on your laptop and write". As with everything, you stuck by me and supported me, never complaining, but offering assistance as I went through the process of getting this done and I thank you, not just for this but for being the awesome husband and person that you are. I am so thankful to God for sending you to me, for you have given me back my smile and made my life beautiful, and I love you with everything I am.

To my wonderful stepchildren, Jason, Jr. and Nia Broux: You two are added treasure to my life. I thank you for the love you've always shown me, the laughs and everything we share. God gave me two new awesome children, including my own little comedian, and my only girl, the daughter I never had. I love you dearly.

And to **YOU**… every mother who has lost a child, and every person who has lost a loved one to a tragic death; THIS BOOK IS WRITTEN TO AND FOR YOU!

Table of Contents

CHAPTER 1

"WOODA WOODA"

On January 2, 1986, at 1:16 p.m., the first of my three sons was born. It was 23 hours earlier that I had what I call my first serious, desperate, heart-to-heart talk with God since being saved years before. The doctor told me that to give birth to a baby only 28 weeks into pregnancy was reason for great concern, because at this stage a baby's heart and lungs are normally not fully developed. He explained that due to readings from monitors that were attached to my abdomen he believed my son's heart to be strong, but he was quite concerned for what the condition of his lungs may be. He then went on to introduce other doctors who were to explain the trouble they were expecting and the not-so-pretty sights I should be prepared to see after my son's birth. It was at that moment the reality set in that this was not a routine, joyful trip to the hospital for childbirth. I closed my eyes, tuned out everyone in the room and began talking to God. At the end of the prayer I declared if I heard him cry, I'd know he will be alright. Hours later this precious, 3lb 3oz baby boy, preciously known to me as my "Wooda Wooda", came screaming into the world, eyes wide opened and holding the keys to my heart. Unlike what the doctors were expecting, he never had to be connected to anything more than a monitor and was perfectly healthy/normal, going home after 3 ½ weeks of merely eating to reach the weight of 5 ½ lbs which at the time was a requirement for a baby to leave the hospital, and being spoiled and adored by the nursing staff.

My life completely transformed being the mother to this wonderful little boy, who from the very beginning was loving, extremely smart, energetic, and full of personality. I can remember so many things from as early as 9 months old to attest to his loving to entertain. He would do funny little things and his face would light up when he realized he'd made someone laugh, especially me. There were many elementary school adventures, and during this period he discovered his love for and talent of drawing. In fact it was during punishment of being confined to his room for 2 hours for one of his adventures that he added his personal touch to the beauty of my home by drawing a large mural in crayon over a portion of his bedroom wall. I will never forget walking in asking if he'd learned his lesson and looking at the big smile on his face after I'd spotted the artwork as he proudly said "see, pretty huh." I also remember how proud I was when at age 7 he told me he wanted to be baptized because he knew that Jesus died for his sins and God raised Him from the dead, and he wanted to sing in the choir and go the Heaven when he dies.

It was so amazing in middle school to see such a transformation begin. Who was this young man with hair on his face, voice deepening, interest in girls, and the desire to drive like fire shut up in his bones? This was also the time period that launched his love for creating music. He and my middle son, Damon, would sit for hours and create melodies, or "beats" as they called them, and write lyrics together. I was still so happy that even with all the changes, his sweet, humble, fun personality remained the same. Then from middle school to high school; he was now taller than I. He begged me to allow him to play football, but regrettably I refused due to fear of him being hurt. Football players as I knew them were all tall, huge guys with necks the size of my thighs. There was no way I was going to let my 5'11, small to medium frame baby get trampled in football, so he resorted to track instead which he developed a love for. It was then that I understood the explanation he was giving about playing football as he showed how fast he was and said "see, they won't catch me to trample on me". He was very good in track and therefore received many plaques and metals, and also had the honor of working as trainer to the girl's track team at his school.

Before we knew it high school graduation was approaching. Where had the time gone? My little WoodaWooda was growing up. I was awestruck as I took notice to the wonderful young man he had become. My once little boy now practically a man, who loved little children and children were crazy about him. Where many his age had no time for the little ones, he enjoyed taking up time with, playing with, teaching and buying them things. I hadn't seen many graduating seniors, especially males who enjoyed attending birthday parties and other celebrations for much younger siblings and family members who may have been only five or six years old. Then came graduation day, which for me was bitter sweet. It was sweet because I was so proud of his accomplishments as well as of the person he had become; bitter because he was growing up and I had to let go of my grip and I wished I could hold on to and continue to shield and protect him forever.

CHAPTER 2

"HE'S A MAN NOW"

Only weeks after graduation Brandon had landed his first job as a sales associate at Mervyn's Department Store. This in essence was his second job, the first one working on weekends in lawn care with his stepfather to experience earning and handling money, as well as to pay for damages to the car he wrecked in middle school during that wildfire urge to drive. He was recognized as employee of the month after only three months of employment, and had already won the hearts of all of his coworkers and customers. I was so touched and proud when after receiving his first paycheck he came to me with the biggest smile, holding not the money, but a gift for me. He remembered I'd wanted a silver ankle bracelet but said I didn't have the money to get one but would someday, and he'd bought one for me (a gift I will keep and cherish always).

In the fall of 2004 while continuing to work at Mervyn's he began attending college full time, taking preliminary courses in pursuit of a degree in architecture. A couple months later, he had saved up enough money to purchase his first vehicle (even after purchasing yet another gift for me, a pair of boots that he also had heard me say I wanted). Oh the smile and look of pride he had as the salesman handed him the keys. With his own transportation, it was much easier for him to get to work, school, and to a friend's studio where he would spend the remainder of his time creating music (when he wasn't up all night creating on the equipment in his room).

Weeks later, he was given a full time job at another company with much nicer pay. I watched him come and go, wondering how in the world he did it, working full time, attending school full time and doing very well with better than a 3.5 GPA, and putting time into music. Most of his money went toward purchases of more and more equipment to create "beats".

I recall one evening while riding in the car with him, he very excitedly said "Mama, I have something I want you to listen to." He put in a cd and let a portion of each track play. He just smiled as I enjoyed the music, clueless to the fact that it was all created by him. When he told me it was his I was joyfully overwhelmed at his talent and creativity. It was then that he told me an award-winning artist wanted to use the music on his next album, and that I could expect to see him on the following year's awards show for his accomplishment.

Shortly after this, partially due to conflict with him not understanding the rule of not coming home at 4:00 a.m. even if I did know where he was and that he wasn't doing anything wrong, he moved out. Still working, attending school, and making music he stayed a short while with one close relative, and then with his father and grandmother, all of whom he discovered had the same rules regarding curfew, or coming in at a decent hour at least. Then he moved into my mother's home not too far away which at the time was being renovated, in order to assist her by monitoring the renovations, as it was difficult for her because at the time she lived in another city. This would also afford him freedom to come and go without disturbing anyone's rules or curfew, yet he was still just within my reach. Again I was pleased that he continued to remain loving, humble, committed to attending church, and stopping to see me most mornings when he got off from work. What will forever be one of my most cherished memories is that of my sleeping early one morning in June of 2005, and trying to turn over but my legs wouldn't move, to open my eyes and realize it was because of him kneeling beside my bed asleep with the top half of his body resting on my lower legs. He had stopped by after working all night as he often did. I smiled and uncomfortably, yet proudly and happily held that position until he awoke, thinking "if he's a man, living alone, working and attending school, has a girlfriend, yet still wants to lay on his Mama's legs and go to sleep, I won't dare make him move."

CHAPTER 3

"DON'T LIKE WHAT I'M SEEING SON"

As weeks went by, Brandon became more and more wrapped up in his music. He was so intrigued by the industry and the money he was making from it. It wasn't long before he informed me he'd decided to put school off for a semester in order to do some things he'd been asked to do in the music arena. He was very excited to inform me that he had made $11,000.00 in one night when a top rap artist bought the beats he had created to use them on his upcoming album (beats were used, artist received awards for songs with his music, but he never received a dime, nor was he even acknowledged).

It was during this time that I was growing worried about Brandon. I knew his heart and saw that he remained committed to doing the right things, but I also knew that he was still very young and inexperienced with dealing with people, and he had a weakness of believing that people aren't that bad and believing everyone was kindhearted as he. It was at this time Brandon began what I call role playing, or "hanging and trying to fit in" with the music makers interested in his work, particularly one accomplished artist who was then affiliated by his fans to violence, drug sales, etc.; once a sort of shy young man who lived around the corner, played ball with my sons, and ate at my table. I told Brandon I didn't like what I was seeing when I noticed the sagging pants, diamond studs in his ears and oversized t-shirts. He assured me that it was just to get his music out there because the artists listening to his beats wouldn't take him seriously if he didn't look like one of them. "I've got to look the part Mama", he said. I was grateful for the explanation as well as the fact that as hard as he tried to fit in, he still stood out like a sore thumb, because his character was far from that of those he was hanging around in the name of making money. My hope was for him to either quickly make his mark and get away from it, or get tired of trying before he too was transformed into someone else. I didn't want him to get caught up in a world of negativity he knew nothing about.

CHAPTER 4

"JULY 4, 2005"

What a beautiful day that was. The weather was perfect; sunny, yet not too hot; no rain in sight. My brother-in-law was having an Independence Day celebration at his home where his large back yard connected to an area park. There was food as far as the eye could see, music, and various games being played by children and adults.

The main attraction for us was the family famous volleyball game. We would often get together and enjoy playing volleyball, sometimes into the night where it was too dark to see the ball. Brandon and I were on the same team on that day, which was quite often the winning team I might add. I recall the two of us being positioned at the net with Brandon next to me, and a rather big and tall gentleman across from me on the other team. Brandon playfully said to him "now don't you mess around and hurt my mama. I don't want to have to hurt you out here". Everyone laughed. My brother-in-law in wanting to win the game was trying to find a way to switch places with me without being detected since it was against the rules of the game. It was the majority's opinion that I wouldn't stand a chance against this gentleman because he was a great deal taller than I and was known for his spike. How shocked they were when the ball was just above the net between us and I jumped up and served him with a mean spike, scoring the point for my team. All were stunned, and when the gentleman asked how in the world I jumped that high Brandon leaned down and pointed to my calves and said "look at that; you think she has these calf muscles for nothing". Everyone practically doubled over in laughter.

I also recall on this day how strange it was when I noticed that Brandon was clinging to me all day. We were always close and he would come to me periodically at these type functions to see if I wanted anything, but he never would stay right next to me as he did this day. At first I thought I may be imagining it so I purposely walked from one end of the yard to the other a few times, and each time I settled he was right next to me. It indeed wasn't my imagination. Then, while I was joking with one of our family members, I looked up and he was gone. My nephew walked up and told me Brandon said to tell me he was leaving. I asked where he was and my nephew pointed to the street a distance away at the opposite end of the park. When I looked up, Brandon was sitting in the driver's seat of his car looking at me, and when I looked at him he slowly turned his head and drove away. This was very strange to me because it was and is a tradition in my family that you kiss everyone bye when leaving. This was the first time Brandon had ever left without hugging/kissing me. I sat for a minute puzzled, staring in that direction even after his car was out of sight, then returned to the celebration but left to go home shortly thereafter.

Once home, my two younger sons, Damon and Justin, were bugging me to get in touch with Brandon because he'd said he was going to come and get them to spend the night with him that night to play video games with them (which he often did). After I'd had all of the badgering I could stand, I began calling Brandon's cell phone but couldn't reach him. The next day I found out he had gone to the small town where my husband was from, which is where he had begun spending much of his free time. He'd explained to me that he liked going there because there were many family members there near his age and they enjoyed cooking out, playing games and having fun together without the threat of violence he had encountered here in the city when he and others would try to find fun things to do. I told the boys that Brandon would more than likely come and get them when he returned, and that I would continue to try and call him so they could talk to him, which I did, but his cell phone was going straight to voicemail.

CHAPTER 5

"THE PHONE CALL"

Wednesday, July 6, 2005 began as a normal day. I prepared meals, watched movies with the boys, etc. One thing that was different though was Damon's and Justin's continuous badgering for me to get in touch with their big brother. As the day before, I called several times but his phone continued to go straight to voicemail. Early that afternoon I found out from one of my in-laws that he was still in the small town and his phone probably had no reception, or the battery could possibly be dead because he had been overheard stating that he had left his charger at home. According to other family members and friends this is what was happening when they'd seen him earlier that day, and that he was to return home that evening. I explained that to the boys and they settled into the fact that he was going to come and get them later that night.

It was a typical evening of watching television, dinner, baths, and getting dressed for bed. I was drying and putting away the dinner dishes at around 9:30 p.m. when the telephone rang. At that moment I froze because a feeling hit me in the pit of my stomach like a bolt of lightning. My husband Jerry answered the phone in the bedroom. I stood still in the kitchen listening to his calm voice talking to the person on the other end, and then hung up. After he didn't say anything I stepped from the kitchen into the hallway that lead to our bedroom and saw him walking toward me. I asked who it was and what was wrong and he said "nothing". I told him that he may as well tell me because I already knew. He then announced that it was his brother who had called, and he said he didn't have any details but Brandon had just been shot and they wanted us to go to the country; a moment I will never forget, that changed my life forever. I called to inform Brandon's father but reached his grandmother instead and informed her of the situation, and said that I'd call as soon as I knew more. I also called my aunt Cynthia, who's also Brandon's Godmother to inform her of the shooting and told her to begin to pray, and that I had no details and would call her as soon as I had more information.

Within minutes we were piled into the car headed to Simmesport, Louisiana. For the duration of the hour long trip that seemed to take 3 that night, I tuned out everything and everyone, with my eyes closed tightly and my head between my knees in the front seat of the car, as I begged and pleaded with God to let my son be alive and not be suffering. I remember during that time that my feelings and prayers would vacillate back and forth between him being ok, imagining him sitting in the back of an EMS unit being treated for a flesh wound to the arm, to a sense that it was far more serious. When the car stopped and Jerry said "we're here", I slowly sat up to see extreme darkness, with what seemed to be a million red lights flashing not very far ahead of us, and a sea of people standing around. As I stepped out of the car, envisioning my son sitting, waiting for me in the back of the EMS unit as they patched his arm, I asked "where is he? Where's my baby?" With the second question I began slightly crying, because I sensed the situation since no one moved. At that moment, people began walking toward me, crowding me saying "oh Rhonda, I'm so sorry".

At that moment I began to scream seemingly from my toes, calling for my beloved son who I then realized had died. Never had I felt such indescribable, agonizing pain so deep. Never had I felt such confusion and weakness, and helplessness. I began to cry out to God, begging Jesus to please help me, and have mercy, and let him come back; take me instead of him. I wanted to go to my son, to see him, because even then I felt he needed me, but I wasn't allowed. Then… came the moment of no words. There are no words to express what I felt next. It was as if I was out of my mind, not knowing what to do, whether to sit or to stand, to scream or to be silent, to throw myself to the ground, or to run. I didn't know what or how to think. It seemed as though I was stuck somewhere in an unknown zone.

Somehow I ended up inside the relative's house Brandon had been visiting, which I later learned was just steps from where he lay; the spot where I'm told he gently smiled and closed his eyes peacefully, as he seemed to sleep away, just steps down the street from where he'd been shot. The house was filled with many in-laws who had also traveled there upon hearing of what happened. I recall many hugs, and sympathetic smiles, and being told "I'm sorry". My husband then asked if I should call my family and tell them what's happened. I called my aunt and informed her, and told her that I would be heading back home shortly. When I hung up from her I told my husband that I don't know if I had the strength to tell my mother, but that I think I'd better tell her, and proceeded to call my mother, who immediately knew something was wrong due to the time of the call, the sound of my voice, and that I was trying to assure she wasn't alone. She began yelling "what's wrong Rhonda; tell me what's wrong Rhonda", when I said "Mommie, Brandon is dead; they killed my child". When I heard her crying "no, no, no", and her voice get faint trying to explain to my stepfather what happened, I could no longer hold the phone.

My friend and cousin-in-law asked that we stay there that night, but I wanted to go home so we left. The ride was very long and silent as I rode hurt, confused, devastated, in disbelief, and stuck in what I call the unknown zone; that place where I don't know how to describe what I was feeling. Arriving home and the rest of that night is a blank to me.

CHAPTER 6

"NO R.I.P'S"

Much of the next day, Thursday, July 7th is a blur to me. I only have flashes of replays of that day. Much of it was spent still in that "unknown zone" of which I became so familiar. I recall family members, coworkers, and friends arriving at my home in an effort to comfort me, yet torn to pieces themselves. I remember bouts of uncontrollable screams and cries, as well as holding on to and hugging Brandon's picture, and staring at it in silence thinking "I'm not going to make it. I can't live past this". I remember waking from medication induced sleep to realize all over again what was happening, and getting angry that I could wake up but my son couldn't. I remember staring at his picture and wondering what was happening to him, as I hadn't seen him, and had been told that I wouldn't be able to see him until the following day, as he had been taken to Lafayette for an autopsy to be performed. This made me feel as a loving mother wanting to accompany and take care of her baby, but prohibited. I recall my split personality, part wanting to die, either in place of or along with my son, and the other wanting to be strong enough to comfort and stay to take care of the two who remain.

By Friday morning I was being carried by what I define as "mama mode". I'd begun thinking and planning what I thought of then as the last thing I could do for my Brandon; my final act of taking care of him. I'd chosen the funeral home whose work I had been quite impressed with, and it had to be nothing but the best for my baby. I'd received a phone call that morning from the DA's office that they were done and he would be transported later that afternoon to where I directed. My focus then had shifted to sorting every detail of how to best honor Brandon.

As I thought of my son, at this point the worst thing that could happen in my opinion was for him to be thought of, viewed, or portrayed as another "street thug" in another black-on-black murder over drugs, or money, or territorial foolishness, which had become so prevalent. I didn't want his wonderful character to be demeaned or undermined in any way, yet, I remained silent because I didn't want others saying that "I was just saying otherwise because I'm his mother". I wanted his true character and the life he had lived to speak for him. Therefore, I asked that no one wear t-shirts with his picture to the funeral as at that time this was associated with elements of society that I didn't want Brandon to be associated with. I also requested that no one spray "RIP" in car windows for the same reason. I also chose all white vehicles for the funeral procession, and selected white as the color of choice to be worn to the funeral because other than his race, there was nothing black about him and this was an angel going to be with the Lord. This was a radiant, beautiful, angelic, uplifting life and I wanted everything about his funeral to be radiant, beautiful, angelic and uplifting in parallel.

Around 3:00 that afternoon, I received the call that he'd arrived at the funeral home and I could come and see him. Against funeral home representative's suggestion and advice, I requested that he not be touched until I arrived: I wanted to see his natural face as it was, not after it had been altered. Many of my family members gathered at the funeral home to accompany me as I embarked upon the hardest thing I've ever had to do; look at my deceased son. I remember the huge lump in my throat and pounding in my chest as I stood outside in the funeral home's parking area attempting to walk toward the door. My aunt Shelia (Shenia as we call her) walked up to me and hugged me as I said "I can't do this. I can't go in there." She replied "you've got to go in there. Come on, we're all going with you". I recall recognizing my son from a distance, lying on the table, and at that moment, "mama mode" kicked in again as I went over to him, hugged him and announced "it's okay man, Mama's here now". I have also recorded the memory of that moment, taking note of the peaceful, slight smile on his face, appearing to be only sleeping, and the small peace inside me that had been assured he didn't suffer.

The next couple of hours were spent choosing the most beautiful casket, flowers, and final resting place available. Brandon's father and I sat together and searched for those things that we felt he would love, keeping his favorite color of blue in mind, sparing no expense. It was this unfortunate time that I understood and appreciated the value of what my husband Jerry had stressed; the need for good life insurance. Over the next several days my mother and I planned the program, wrote tributes, and selected snow white attire that we, my family, and Brandon would wear. Then after I was satisfied that every detail had been taken care of in what I felt to be the final thing I can do for my wonderful son, including purchasing a blue teddy bear for him that would wear a customized jersey in his Belaire High School colors, bearing my name for him, "Wooda Wooda", the "unknown zone" returned, adding that I wanted to withdraw and be alone and silent, as I counted down the days and hours to the day I'd say goodnight to my son, and see his face no more in this life.

Saturday, July 16, 2005 was a gorgeous, sunny day, but our and many other hearts were heavy, and spirits were filled with gloom. I recall the neighbors outside smiling as they saw the beautiful long white limousines. I remember hearing in a distance one of them ask a family member who's getting married, and someone answered, "no, she's going to bury her son". The memories of that day from that point on are spliced and scattered; family members and my pastor in the receiving room; walking to our seats; some of the songs and words spoken by those on program. I recall an isolated moment where I looked around and took notice of the many, many attendees, and thinking "wow…how in the world did he know this many people and touch this many lives in such a short time". I remember the pride I felt at that moment, along with the shame of thinking "if he's touched all of these people in 19 short years, I better get on my job and catch up." I recall at some point thinking to myself that I'd always said I never wanted to sit in that seat (the front row of a funeral due to death of a close relative), and there I was. I also recall thinking, reasoning right after that about which seat I'd prefer to sit in, this one, the seat of a mother of a wonderful son who had continued to proclaim his salvation and love for Jesus Christ, so now in paradise with the Lord, or the seat the mother of the man who killed him, knowing her son had taken a life, then that of an innocent child practically, and he would spend the remainder of his life in prison. It was at that moment that I said to myself that I proudly and thankfully take my seat. The remainder of my recollections of that day include the dreaded moment just before the casket was closed, begging them to wait because I wouldn't see his face again, the sealing of the mausoleum, and drifting at the repast as I watched people hover over and hoard food. The remainder of that and days after are a complete blank besides the thoughts of trying to figure how I would go on from this point.

CHAPTER 7

"LORD HELP ME!"

The funeral was over, nothing left to do. The phone calls slowed, and the wave of visitors receded. In the quiet time with nothing else to plan or think about, and no visitors to look at or listen to, the realization of the previous two weeks settled. I recall lying on my bed and looking at Brandon's picture, and realizing….this is not a dream; he's really not here anymore; I really just laid my son to rest! Immediately the gut-wrenching pain took over again, along with the feeling of not knowing how I would take my next breath, or make it past this point. I grabbed my bible and hugged it snugly, but couldn't focus enough to read it, so I just closed my eyes and begged God to help me, as I knew that the only way I could go on would be with His help and strength.

It seemed as though everything was strange and wrong now; like everything was changed and out of place. With confusion and uncertainty of how I would continue to live it seemed as though I had actually moved to a strange place, in the middle of that "unknown zone" which existed in a strange time and space. I am so thankful though that in the midst of my insanity, I did have the wherewithal and the knowing deep within my spirit of where my help lie; in none other than Jesus Christ. This is why when I could, nor wanted to think any other thought or say any other word, I would think or say "Lord, I need You to help me." In the middle of wishing I wouldn't wake up for feeling guilty because I was still alive but my 19-year-old son wasn't, there remained an awareness within me that I still had two other sons here that needed me; that I had to raise. Of course I felt as I believe all loving mothers do, that no one will take care of them like I. This caused me again and again to say, "Lord, please help me." I didn't want to eat. I didn't want to sleep. I didn't want to talk to anyone. I didn't want to go anywhere. I definitely didn't want the three medicines the doctor had prescribed. But I did want and knew I needed God to help me. I understood, even in the midst of this storm, that the only way I would be able to take my next breath, or once breathing to continue doing what I need to do in this life, or to just remain, God would have to help me. It was somewhere between this knowing and my feeling God's help that *Acts 17:28* became my very favorite scripture, for it definitely *"is in Him that I live, and move, and have my being."*

CHAPTER 8

"STRIKE-A-BLOW"

Due to the fact that my son's murderer was arrested on the same night of his death, it didn't take very long for legal proceedings, trial, etc. to begin. I shifted my focus to closely monitoring the progress of the case in order to do whatever possible to assure justice for my son, as well as make certain the DA understood that this was not "just another black on black crime between two thugs over drugs or territory". My son was no "street nigger" and was not caught up into any behavior that in this society would possibly warrant his death. I remember the disgust I felt when I could sense that this was the feeling, as well as the relief and pride I felt when I received the phone call from the DA informing me of court dates, etc., and hearing the change in his voice and attitude because he'd found out a little about Brandon, and realized "he was just a good kid", as well as hearing his wife sobbing in the background saying from all she's heard this was just senseless and if they could do anything for me let them know and call her anytime if I wanted to talk.

By now I'd heard quite similar stories of what had taken place on the evening prior to as well as the evening of my son's murder. I'd heard that it was known that my son would sleep on a sofa near the front door of a friend's home when he stayed in that town. I'd heard that on the evening of July 5th the man who murdered my son, along with his cousin whom my son had known, yet wasn't aware disliked him, came to the house that night and asked for a ride across the river, but my son told them he only had enough gas to make it back home; an occurrence that leads me to believe Brandon was suspicious of the two due to the fact it was later noted he had a full tank of gas. I'd also heard that later that night, the same individual was seen supposedly attempting to steal Brandon's car from the yard, but only moved it a few feet down the street and left it there; what's believed to have been a second attempt to lure him outside the house.

In addition to the things I'd heard about the previous night, there were also corroborating stories regarding the events of the dreadful day of his murder. I'd heard that Brandon had promised some of the neighborhood kids and younger cousins that he would bring them a copy of the music he had recorded, and he, loving kids as he did, drove home to Baton Rouge, retrieved copies of the CDs and brought them back. Just after he returned some of the kids asked him to drive them to the store which he did, and upon returning and attempting to walk down the street towards his cousin's house, he was approached by the same two, who were then lying await in the bushes. Then it was said that "Strike-A-Blow" (pronounced "strikuh blow") which is the nickname of the 27-year-old known criminal that shot my son walked up to him and said "I guess you're gona be looking for me now" (referring to the fact that there was much talk that he'd been seen trying to steal Brandon's car), and put a gun to his chest and pulled the trigger. It was also stated that he remained lurking around the area after my son's death, even standing with the crowd watching me, as I screamed for my son, and commenting "she may as well shut up all that screaming, the nigga dead now". Thanks to witness statements he was arrested within the hour.

The trial was very short. There are several memories engraved in my mind regarding the trial. One was of "Strike-A-Blow's" sorely weeping mother, who looked at him calling his name and asking why, and looking at me and apologizing repeatedly. I remember taking the stand to make a statement to the killer, informing him that he did not hurt Brandon, but he hurt me and all of his family members and friends present in court and the many others who couldn't attend, as well as telling him that he was correct in that the third teardrop tattoo (said to represent a murder) he had just added being the largest, because with spending the rest of his life in jail for the death of Brandon Dwayne Chatman would be the biggest tear he ever cries. I remember becoming very irritated at the fact that he wouldn't look at me; I wanted him to look me in my face, and he wouldn't. He would look at and sometimes even smirk at everyone else, yet he would not look at me. Then came the two best memories; hearing the judge sentence him to life, hard labor in prison without benefit of parole, probation, or appeal, and after court embracing his mother telling her that I am more sorry for her, then hearing the defense attorney say that this is the type of case that makes her hate her job because she'd traveled to Baton Rouge and surrounding areas, as well as ordered extensive tests of Brandon's blood in search of anything negative regarding him to help her case, and for the first time in her career, she could find absolutely nothing and no one with a negative word to say about him.

CHAPTER 9

"NOW WHAT?"

In the first months following the trial I was in sort of a solemn place. The funeral was done, the trial was over, and I found myself drifting, wondering where to go from here. Though the pain was still excruciating, and it was all still hard to believe, I realized then I was in fact still alive and therefore wondered "what must I do now." I felt as though I'd been dropped from a spaceship from the "unknown zone" and had to become familiar with my surroundings again. It was the first small glimpse of being able to say "okay, yes I'm still hurting and devastated, however I'm still here, and I still have two sons who need me" and I mustered a little strength to begin going through motions of helping to take care of them. For me this was as a very faint light in the horizon; the first feeling of being able to breathe again.

I spent a lot of quiet moments during this time, reflecting, pondering; thinking. I recall reflecting on Brandon, his smile, laughs we shared, his personality, and most of all how much he loved his Mama. Brandon's love for me, how he hated to see me cry or upset, and the fact that I know he wants me happy and moving forward helps to keep me going (I let him help me). I also began to reflect on God, and how much He loves me, and that He's been with me and has seen me through up to this point, and I recall God's word; *He will never leave me, nor forsake me (Hebrews 13:5); Cast my cares upon Him, for He cares for me (1 Peter 5:7); He who dwells in the secret place of the Most High shall abide under the shadow of the Almighty (Psalm 91:1); He is the same yesterday, today, and forever more (Hebrews 13:8).* This was as the first dose of a multivitamin to give me strength (I let God help me!).

It was also in this time that I knew I wanted to somehow cause some good to come out of this. I didn't know how, what, or where, but I knew I wanted to honor Brandon's life by somehow making someone's life better as a result of the loss of his. I knew this is what he would want as well, to help somebody. I began thinking of his interests and how to help someone in any of them. I began thinking of the young man who was a known mean drug dealer who decided to change his life as a result of seeing "this lil innocent dude who didn't do nothing to nobody but try to help people lose his life," and wonder how to use Brandon's death to help others become saved. I was in a place where I wanted to do something, but didn't know what, as well as needed to begin again with my day to day life, and even with this stood saying "now what?"

CHAPTER 10

"IN SEARCH OF PEACE"

When I finally reached the point where I would actually begin to put the pieces of my life together again and begin moving forward, I realized something was blocking me; holding me back. All of the physical activities were over, I'd had realization time, time to reflect and quiet time. I'd at least arrived at the point I realized I must go on, but somehow I couldn't. No matter what I tried, or how I tried to think or feel, or what I tried to do, there was turmoil or unsettling within. Then, during a moment of what I call relapse I realized what had been missing.

This moment came during one of the many times where Brandon's death and the pain of it seemed so fresh. I missed him and longed to see him and hear his voice, and couldn't believe he was actually gone. I stretched out on my living room floor and wailed in agony in fetal position with my eyes closed, holding on to his picture crying and loudly pleading "I want my baby back; I want him BACK!" It was at that moment that I clearly heard the Holy Spirit ask "wasn't it you who always proclaimed if you never get anything else in this world, you want the best for your children? What does he have now? You want to take that away from him?" I then stopped crying, got up, wiped my face, walked to the bathroom, looked at myself in the mirror, and said "you selfish heffa. According to the Word he's in paradise now, and you want him to come back here to this sinful, hard world? You want to take that from him?" At this point I walked out, apologized to Brandon, and received the small, inner calm that entered. I now know what was missing. I will never be happy about my son's death, and I could definitely never be glad it happened, but at that moment I had a peace about it, at least accepting the fact that God's Word says he has better now than imaginable, and I hold on to and rest in that peace.

I sat then and thought of him and his life, from newborn all the way through his funeral. This pondering gave me a bit more peace. I remembered his funeral, and all of the guestbook entries, and the many people young and old I'd run into who recognized me and told me they knew him and how he'd impacted their lives. During this recollection I grasped what I call the fact that he graduated early. I was amazed at all he had done and the lives he had touched in those short 19 years, and I then felt his life indeed was not stolen from him; he finished early. What parent would be told that their ninth grader has fulfilled everything to graduate from high school, and high school has nothing further to offer would be upset about the child graduating early and beg for them to be allowed to stay? I believe the answer would be none. This is another way God gave me peace about my son's death, and that peace helps to give me strength to endure and move on. I also came away from these two experiences feeling that contrary to what I'd always heard, it indeed is okay to ask God questions, because I asked and He answered. The bible even tells us *that "if any lack wisdom, let him ask of God (James 1:5)."*

The final portion of peace I received, which was also the hardest came as a result of forgiveness. I had to truly forgive the man who killed my son, or the unforgiveness, anger and bitterness would only keep me in inner turmoil. In thinking of the type person Brandon was, he would've had it no other way, and in even the model prayer we ask that God "forgive us, **as we forgive those** who trespass against us". So, I realized that if I want God to forgive me of my sins, then I have to forgive him in the same way. Once I did this, and realized that it's for God and not me to deal with him, I was able to forgive him and experience a little more peace.

CHAPTER 11

"STRENGTHENED FOR SERVICE (I FEEL MY HELP COMING)"

So....., now you know my story. After much pondering and much prayer I decided to share my story in order to help others who have the awesome task of traveling this rugged, life-altering path. I spent many days, years even, pleading with God, asking what can I do, because I truly believe God and His Word, so I believe "*all things* *work together for good to them that love God, to them who are the called according to his purpose (Romans 8:28)*, so I believed with all of my heart that somehow, some good can happen as a result of something so horrible; my son's death.

I remember quite well when the answer to that question came. It was on one of the days when it was heaviest on my mind and heart. I replayed in my mind like a slideshow some of the events surrounding my son's death, the months following, and some period after that. Then there was the memory of my only encounter with another mother I knew who had experienced the same tragedy before I did. This part stood out like a sore thumb as I remembered briefly talking to her, asking her a question, hearing her answer along with her repeating several thoughts that I too had experienced, thinking no one could have thought or felt that besides me. I remembered the

~ 33 ~

sense of energy and ray of hope I felt to hear that someone really does understand and feels what I feel; the bit of strength I gained to see....she's making it, so I can too.

It was at this moment that I thought "yes, that's it! What better way to use this tragedy for good than to help others dealing with a tragic loss of death to walk through it; sharing with them the path I took (and am still taking) to endure, comforting them with our shared feelings and thoughts, offering them a ray of hope through my experiences, and letting them see that if I can make it, so can they." Thus this journey began. Since then I've felt a compelling urgency, desire and duty to run to any mother that tragically loses a child or anyone who loses someone to a tragic death, and along with it a greater sense of God's strength and power with me. Therefore now, *"I must be about my Father's business" (Luke 2:49).*

CHAPTER 12

"Q AND A"

I decided to end with a question and answer (Q&A) section in hopes of assisting with answers to some questions that really helped me, as well as put your minds at ease by possibly exposing some quite common thoughts and feelings that you may have been believing only you've had. I've also included biblical clarifications of statements made by what I believe to be well-meaning individuals attempting to comfort bereaved families/individuals. I have tried to answer the main question of how I've made it thus far step by step throughout the pages of this book, which ultimately points to a total trust and dependency upon God and His word.

Questions

<u>Should I be mad at God</u>? No, because God didn't do anything; the devil did. The bible says "the devil comes to kill, steal, and destroy, but I (God) have come that you may have life and have it more abundantly." Because He has ultimate power, God had to allow it, but He only even allows things with a turn out for a good part of His ultimate plan. The devil is the one to be mad at.

Is this punishment for something I did; is it my fault? Absolutely not. If God wanted to punish you, He would punish YOU, not take the life of someone else. PEOPLE often make the vicious statement that in order for bad things to happen, someone must have done something wrong or sinned. The answer to this is also taught in scripture whereby *Jesus passes a blind man, and His disciples asked who sinned, him or his parents causing him to be blind, and Jesus told them that no one had sinned, but it was so the works of God should be made manifest or shown in him (John 9:1-3)*, meaning that sometimes seemingly negative situations occur in order for God to make known His power that's available for this and other situations. If we never needed, witnessed or experienced God's power, we would never understand just what He's made available to us. The bible also lets us know that God is a much better parent than we know how to be (Matthew 7:11)), so would you take the life of one of your children in order to punish another, or to teach another a lesson? Of course not. Therefore, God definitely wouldn't.

Is it wrong for me to cry, or does crying make me weak or less of a Christian? Certainly not. Crying is a natural reaction to pain, and I believe provides a release to the pressure of dealing with pain. Jesus is our ultimate role model and example, so if *"Jesus wept" (John 11:35)* at the death of His friend, why wouldn't we? There is a difference in crying with hopeless doom, but we as Christians can cry because we are hurt at the loss of someone we love. *"Do not sorrow **as those who have no hope**" (1 Thessalonians 4:13)*. Crying is also a part of grieving. Please note that in order to heal, YOU MUST ALLOW YOURSELF TIME TO GRIEVE. Suppressing it and going about daily life as if nothing's happened does not help, but will slowly eat away at you on the inside like a cancer and will show itself in some negative way later. Everyone is different, and therefore may grieve in different ways. Know what yours are and allow yourself to do it. You will know by the relief, comfort, and gradual helping to better cope that comes about as a result.

<u>Is it strange that it sometimes still doesn't seem real, or I have to stop and think that this really did happen</u>? No, it's not. In devastating situations such as this, I believe our minds have a built-in mechanism that prevents us from dwelling on the situation because our minds couldn't handle that type pressure, so it makes sense that ever so often when significant thought of the situation does come up, it's almost as if we have to be reminded that it actually happened, or wasn't a dream. I also believe that because we wish so much that it hadn't happened, our minds get caught up in that and the fact that it actually did. Additionally, I believe that the unexpectedness of it plays a key part in this. Though it doesn't hurt any less, or mean that you love others any less, it seems to add just a bit more pain or edge when death is sudden and tragic than if it could have been expected like with extended illness, etc. There are still times when I look at my son's picture and find myself saying "wow, this really did happen".

<u>Is it normal to go a stretch of time ok, and then find myself crying again</u>? Absolutely. Once you begin to heal the burden gets lighter little by little, and you cry less often as time goes by. However, because time doesn't erase the fact that you still love and miss your loved one, it's normal to sometimes cry when you think of them, even if you may not have cried for a while.

<u>Should I feel this happened for a reason</u>? The only REASON you should feel this happened is the fact that the devil is real, does have SOME power, and *"comes but to steal, kill, and destroy" (John 10:10)*. However you can rest assure that God is omnipotent (has ALL power), and therefore would only have allowed it for good purpose. I'm reminded, for example, of a quarterback I saw on television once who talked about an accident as a boy whereby his pinky finger was broken, and could never be set to where it was back to normal. He's a quarterback in the NFL due to that finger giving him an edge on the way in which he can throw the ball. (The devil set the trap to tragically break a boy's finger beyond repair, but God said, "go on and break it", and gave the boy a specially designed tool to becoming a millionaire doing something he loves to do.)

<u>Is it ok for me to want to be alone, or to not want to be alone</u>? Either is just fine; whatever you need to heal is what you must do. The only thing to watch for is that you don't allow wanting to be alone to become being totally withdrawn and depressed, and you don't want to become dependent upon being with others. But it's totally fine and

normal to sometimes want to be alone, and to sometimes want to be with others and not alone.

<u>Should I feel guilty that I'm here and he's/she's not</u>? Absolutely not. I realize we feel this way periodically out of love, and feel somehow that it's unfair that we were allowed to remain here, especially if it's your son or daughter or someone younger. But the truth of the matter is if it were meant for it to be that way, it would've happened that way. Therefore, there is no reason to feel guilty.

<u>Is it ok for me to create ways that I feel I'm in his/her presence or close to him/her (looking at picture, holding a favorite item, etc.)</u>? Definitely. The whole thing of missing someone is longing to be close to them, so if you have something that comforts you by making you feel close to them it should do nothing but make the journey a little better. I often talk to my son's picture, touch some of his things that I have that I know he touched, hug the teddy bear that sat next to him during the funeral, just little things to feel that physical point of contact that I'm missing.

<u>What about counseling</u>? Just as in the previous question, you should do whatever YOU need to do to help heal you and make you feel better. The answer to this question is totally based upon each individual. If it lingers and there are things you just can't seem to get past, then I believe counseling would only be a plus. Then there are others who already know that they normally benefit from talking to others so for you counseling may be employed from the beginning.

Then there are they who may not need counseling but heal by other means. I personally did not seek counseling. One thing I firmly believe though is that in some cases a close relationship with God and His word works without counseling. But I would never rely on counseling to work without God.

Should I try to forget? I say remember your loved one, the things that made you smile, the details of their life, and the good memories you have, but by all means forget the details of the tragedy and anything that only causes you pain.

Statements

God came and picked a flower; He only takes the best. The bible tells us that *"He came that we may have life, and have it more abundantly" (John 10:10)*, and that *"He will satisfy us with long life" (Psalm 91:16)* as a blessing of obedience. Therefore why would He then lie in wait to come and pick off the best? Or what would be motivation for us striving to be the best or more like Jesus if it's just to be "taken away"?

God needed a _?_ in Heaven so he took them. The bible teaches us that *"God created the heaven and the earth" (Genesis 1:1)*, and *"He is the same yesterday, today, and forevermore" (Hebrews 13:8)*, so He still has power to create or speak into being, as He did before, anything He wants in Heaven, so there is absolutely no need for Him to come here (causing death and pain) to look for anything He would desire in Heaven.

Be strong; Don't cry. As I stated in an earlier chapter, Jesus is our ultimate role model and example of strength, therefore, if *"Jesus wept" (John 11:35)* at the death of Lazarus, whom by the way He knew He would call from the grave, and *"groaned in the spirit and was troubled" (John 11:33)*, why then would we be expected not to? Christians are instructed to *"not sorrow as those who have no hope" (1 Thessalonians 4:13)*, but are not instructed not to weep for the pain of losing someone we love.

God won't put no more on you than you can bear. I've been hearing this statement for as long as I can remember, However, I have learned that God doesn't put anything on us. He said *"come unto me all who labor and are heavy laden and I will give you rest" (Matthew 11:28)*, and He sent His son Jesus to bear the weight of our sins on the cross. Why would He say and do this just in order to turn around and put something on us to bear. Who would want to serve a God that you sit around and wait for to put something on us to bear? Again, the bible teaches that "we being evil know how to treat our children" and we do all we can to prevent things from happening to them, so would God who is incomparably above/better than us do the opposite and cause things to happen to His children? (Matthew 7:11) Sure he may allow things that feel bad to us that we don't understand right now. But if we know that God **is** a good God, then we have to trust and know that though it doesn't feel good, it must've been allowed **for** good. Sort of the way we give our children horrible tasting medicine knowing the outcome, or take them to the doctor for immunizations to receive a painful shot and they're not sick; though they don't understand it, we know it's part of our plan for good or for their protection.

I am very grateful, honored and humbled to have had the opportunity to share my story with you, and it is my sincere hope and prayer that something said is a blessing in your life, bringing about comfort, clarity, healing to your soul, and change for the better. Remember, "*in all these things, we are more than conquerors through Him that loved us" (Romans 8:37)*! As for me, "*I WILL bless the Lord at ALL times; His praise shall **continually** be in my mouth" (Psalm 34:1)*.

Printed in Great Britain
by Amazon